Date: 1/21/22

BR 599.24 NIL
Nilsen, Genevieve,
Wombat joeys /

TOOLS FOR CAREGIVERS

- **F&P LEVEL:** D
- **WORD COUNT:** 56

- **CURRICULUM CONNECTIONS:** animals, habitats

Skills to Teach

- **HIGH-FREQUENCY WORDS:** a, has, in, is, it, the, they, this, with
- **CONTENT WORDS:** baby, back, burrow, claws, digs, faces, fur, grows, joey, live(s), looks, Mom, out, pouch, walks, wombat
- **PUNCTUATION:** periods
- **WORD STUDY:** long /e/, spelled y (baby, joey); long /o/, spelled ow (burrow, grows); /ow/, spelled ou (out, pouch)
- **TEXT TYPE:** factual description

Before Reading Activities

- Read the title and give a simple statement of the main idea.
- Have students "walk" through the book and talk about what they see in the pictures.
- Introduce new vocabulary by having students predict the first letter and locate the word in the text.
- Discuss any unfamiliar concepts that are in the text.

After Reading Activities

Explain to readers that wombats live in the Outback. Temperatures can get very warm. To escape the heat, wombats dig holes in the ground. These are called burrows. Wombats live in them to stay cool and to escape bigger animals that may try to eat them. What other animal homes can readers think of? Why do they think those animals need homes in the wild?

Tadpole Books are published by Jump!, 5357 Penn Avenue South, Minneapolis, MN 55419, www.jumplibrary.com

Copyright ©2022 Jump!. International copyright reserved in all countries. No part of this book may be reproduced in any form without written permission from the publisher.

Editor: Jenna Gleisner **Designer:** Molly Ballanger

Photo Credits: imageBROKER/Alamy, cover, 2tr, 2mr, 4–5; Bennymarty/Dreamstime, 1; Suzi Eszterhas/Minden Pictures/SuperStock, 2bl, 3; NHPA/SuperStock, 2tl, 6–7, 12–13; Dave Watts/Alamy, 8–9; Jonas Boernicke/Shutterstock, 2br, 10–11; Johner Images/Alamy, 2ml, 14–15; Zoe Ezzy/Shutterstock, 16.

Library of Congress Cataloging-in-Publication Data
Names: Nilsen, Genevieve, author.
Title: Wombat joeys / by Genevieve Nilsen.
Description: Minneapolis: Jump, Inc., 2022. | Series: Outback babies | Includes index. | Audience: Ages 3–6
Identifiers: LCCN 2020046245 (print) | LCCN 2020046246 (ebook) | ISBN 9781645279525 (hardcover)
ISBN 9781645279532 (paperback) | ISBN 9781645279549 (ebook)
Subjects: LCSH: Wombats—Infancy—Juvenile literature.
Classification: LCC QL737.M39 N55 2022 (print) | LCC QL737.M39 (ebook) | DDC 599.2/41392—dc23
LC record available at https://lccn.loc.gov/2020046245
LC ebook record available at https://lccn.loc.gov/2020046246

OUTBACK BABIES

WOMBAT JOEYS

by Genevieve Nilsen

TABLE OF CONTENTS

WORDS TO KNOW

burrow

claws

digs

fur

joey

pouch

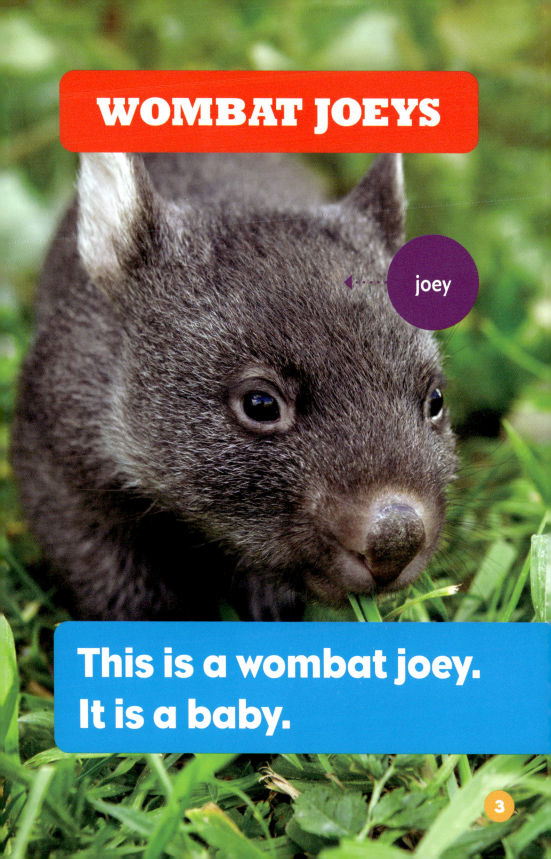

WOMBAT JOEYS

joey

**This is a wombat joey.
It is a baby.**

3

fur

It has fur.

claw

It has claws.

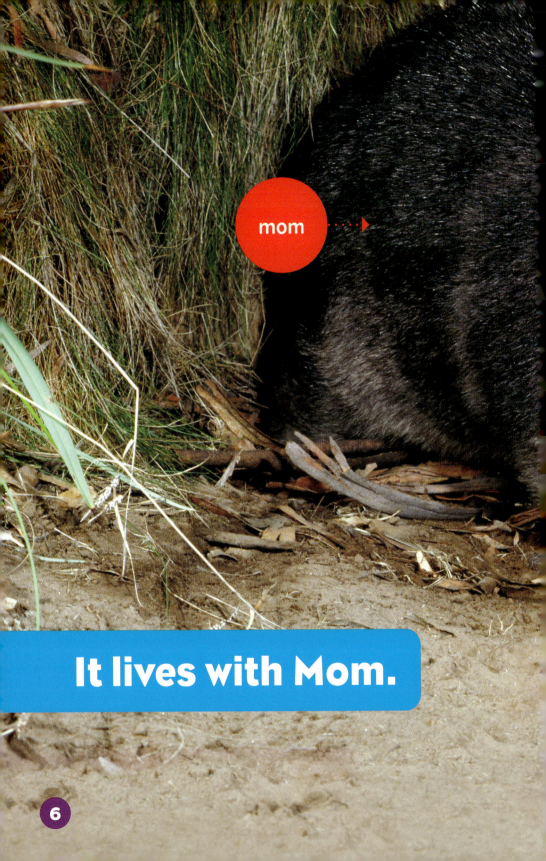

mom

It lives with Mom.

burrow

They live in a burrow.

pouch

Mom has a pouch.

The joey is in it.

The pouch faces back.

pouch

The joey looks out.

The joey grows.

It walks with Mom.

It digs.

It digs a burrow.

LET'S REVIEW!

What are this wombat joey and mom doing?

INDEX